Business Analysis
Defined!

Learn what Business Analysis is,
when to do it in Agile and Waterfall SDM,
and what techniques are in use

Thomas Hathaway
Angela Hathaway

Ordering Information:

Quantity sales. Special discounts are available on quantity purchases by corporations, associations, and others. For details, contact the publisher at books@BusinessAnalysisExperts.com.

The content of this book is also available as an eCourse at businessanalysisexperts.com/product/video-course-business-analysis-defined

ISBN: 1508829977
ISBN-13: 978-1508829973

DEDICATION

This work is dedicated to future generations of Business Analysts, BA Managers, BA Practice Leaders, BA Development Supervisors, Business Architects, Business Consultants, Business Excellence Leads, Business Process Analysts, Business Process Managers, Business Relationship Managers, Business Rule Architects, Business Rules Analysts, Business Specialists, Business Services Managers, Business Strategists, Business Systems Analysts, Change Professionals, CIOs, Continuous Improvement Managers, Directors of Risk Management & Operations , Enterprise Architects, Enterprise Analysis Managers, Functional Analysts, Information Technology Specialists, IT Application Analysts, IS Architects, IT Business Analysts, IT Project Managers, IT Solutions Managers, IT Systems Analysts, Operations Managers, Operations Risk Managers, Product Managers, Project Managers, Program Managers, Quality Control Managers, Requirements Analysis Managers, SOA Engineers, Solution Architects, System Consultants and any other title organizations choose in the future to bestow upon the one wearing the Business Analysis hat (and to http://www.buildingbusinesscapability.com from whom we stole this fine list of titles!).

CONTENTS

Thomas and Angela Hathaway

ACKNOWLEDGMENTS

This publication would not have been possible without the active support and hard work of our daughter, Penelope Hathaway. Many of the ideas in the book started with those who brought us into the field that is now known as business analysis, in particular Dan Myers and Stacy Goff. Our thinking has been greatly influenced by the seeds they planted many moons ago.

We would also be remiss if we did not acknowledge the thousands of students and practicing business analysts with whom we have had the honor of working over the years. We can honestly say that every single one of you influenced us in no small way. It is from that knowledge base that we recognized that business analysis is performed in many organizations by many people with many titles. You also helped us recognize that business analysis is not a simple activity that organizations need every now and then but an on-going process of evaluating where you are today and deciding where you want to be tomorrow.

Finally, we would like to acknowledge Harvey, that fictional Pooka created by Mary Chase and made famous by the movie of the same name with James Stewart. Very early in our marriage we recognized that a third entity is created and lives whenever we work closely on a concept, a new idea, or a new product. Over the years, this entity became so powerful and important to us that we decided to name it Harvey and he should rightfully be listed as the author of this and all of our creative works. Unfortunately, Harvey remains an invisible being, living somewhere beyond our physical senses but real nonetheless. Without Harvey, neither this book nor any of our other publications would have been possible. For us, Harvey embodies the entity that any collaborative effort creates and he is at least as real as each of us. We would truly be lost without him.

Thomas and Angela Hathaway

PREFACE

The content of this book was neither created "For Dummies®" nor "For Complete Idiots®" but for normal people in the real world to give them a basic understanding of some core business analysis methods and concepts. If reading this book answers some of your questions, great. If it raises more questions than it answers (implying that it piqued your curiosity), even better. If it motivates you to learn more about this emerging and fascinating topic, it has served its purpose well.

Although the field of Business Analysis offers great career opportunities for those seeking employment, some level of business analysis skill is essential for any adult in the business world today. Many of the techniques used in the field evolved from earlier lessons learned in systems analysis and have proven themselves to be useful in every walk of life. We have personally experienced how business analysis techniques help even in your private life (more in our 3-part blog post starting at http://businessanalysisexperts.com/business-analysis-techniques-work-1/). This book is a brief introduction to the field and defines business analysis as it is currently practiced, what "requirements" really are, and what techniques those practicing business analysis use. Teaching how to perform each technique far exceeds the scope of this publication.

Meanwhile, please enjoy this Book. We appreciate any comments, suggestions, recommended improvements, or complaints that you care to share with us. You can reach us via email at:

Books@BusinessAnalysisExperts.com.

Thomas and Angela Hathaway

1 WHAT IS BUSINESS ANALYSIS

Questions answered in this chapter:

- What is the purpose of business analysis?
- Why is business analysis gaining importance?

Business Analysis – a Definition

Business analysis is the business process of assessing an organization's structure, processes, technology, and capabilities to identify and define solutions to roadblocks that impede the achievement of organizational goals.

Business Analysis enables adaptation in an ever-changing business and regulatory environment to allow the organization to grow in the manner defined by management.

Although an expanding cadre of "Business Analysts" exists, business analysis is often performed by people with job titles such as "Product Owner", "CEO", "Developer", "Product Manager", "Project Manager", "SME" and many others. More and more organizations recognize the value of business analysis skills for employees in any position.

The key to ensuring that business analysis is a positive force for change is that people doing it have the appropriate skills and techniques to do it well. Whether those individuals have the title "Business Analyst" is a question of the organizational structure, as bestowing the title does not inherently ensure the quality of the outcome. For simplicity, we use the phrase "THE BA" in this book to refer to anyone wearing the business analysis hat, whether or not that individual has the job title Business Analyst.

What Does Business Analysis Entail?

> Business analysis encompasses all activities
> necessary to study the entire organization or
> a specific unit thereof to identify business problems
> and define suitable solutions, often involving an
> Information Technology (IT) component.

To put it differently, business analysis is all about doing whatever it takes to elicit, discover, capture, gather, draw forth, trawl for, flush out, or get requirements for the solution by any means possible implying that requirements are not just lying around waiting to be picked up but require significant effort to help the business community figure out what they need and want. Does that not sound simple?

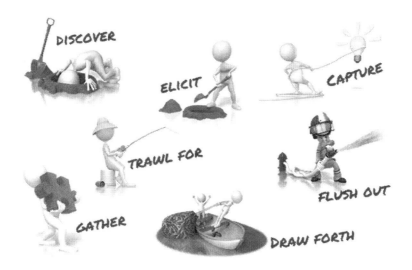

On the other hand, that definition contained 65 words and requires a double doctorate to understand (according to its readability index). OK, maybe it's not so simple.

Oh by the way, all of those activities were just to recognize the requirements. The tasks of analyzing those requirements, expressing them in a manner that the IT professionals could understand them, documenting them, prioritizing them, communicating them, validating them, managing changes in the requirements throughout the project life cycle, working effectively with both Agile and traditional Software Development Methodologies (SDM), and a few other minor activities are obviously natural skills that anyone wearing the business analysis hat brings to the table.

Strategic, Tactical, and Operational Business Analysis

Due to the evolution of the external and internal environments of an organization, change is a fact of life. As a result, business analysis is an on-going activity and organizations use it at **3 major levels** of detail.

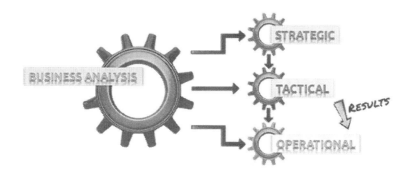

At the enterprise level, **Strategic Business Analysis** expresses executive business goals, objectives, strategies, and visions in the form of Agile Themes and Epics or traditional Project Scope and Business Requirements.

This level encompasses all of the pre-project work of identifying business problems, defining business opportunities, developing a business case, and determining whether to initiate a project. The primary impact your organizational Software Development Methodology (SDM) will have at this level is in how you express the outcomes. In Agile, the results will form the seed for a Product Backlog as a cornerstone of Agile Software Development. For traditional methodologies, the results will be project charters and scope documents. Strategic Business Analysis deals with identifying all conditions and problems that projects should address to affect the change. Without solid enterprise analysis results, there is no basis for a project.

Tactical Business Analysis takes whatever results Strategic Business Analysis delivers to the next level of detail. This level depends on the SDM and on the relative size and complexity of the project.

At this level, business analysis:

☑ identifies impacted stakeholders

☑ captures their individual concerns

☑ elicits stakeholder requirements

☑ conducts feasibility analysis

☑ analyzes and prioritizes the requirements

☑ and manages changing requirements throughout the life of the project

This is the level most commonly associated with **"classic business analysis"** and is heavily dependent on the SDM. In a "Waterfall" project, you will put a major effort up front in defining a clear and complete set of requirements for the entire project. In Agile, you only need high-level business and stakeholder requirements at the beginning and the premise is you will delve in the sufficient level of detail when developers are ready to start coding.

Operational Business Analysis is the third level. As input, it uses the results of Tactical Business Analysis, whether they are expressed as traditional Stakeholder Requirements or in the form of Agile User Stories. It creates Solution Functional Requirements (SFR) and Non-Functional Requirements (NFR).

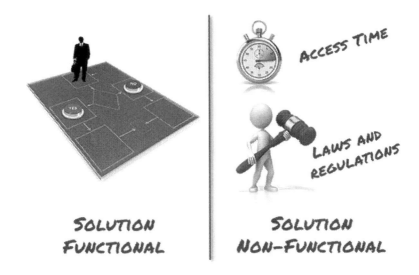

SOLUTION
FUNCTIONAL

SOLUTION
NON-FUNCTIONAL

In an Agile SDM, the development team often performs whatever Operational Business Analysis it needs and only calls on a professional business analyst when the situation warrants it. In traditional SDMs, this level of analysis is completed to the greatest degree possible during the Analysis phase, whereas it is recognized that some Operational Business Analysis is impossible until the design has been worked out.

In today's wired world, most organizations use packaged software for non-strategic applications. Given the nature of packaged applications, the primary purpose of Operational Business Analysis becomes to refine the organization's workflows and procedures to take advantage of the features of the installed package. As the organization's needs change, Operational Business Analysis techniques determine how to adjust those workflows and procedures to achieve the project goal while still taking advantage of the features of the package.

All three levels of business analysis share techniques such as:

☑ problem definition

☑ problem analysis

☑ requirements specification

☑ requirements elicitation

☑ requirements analysis

☑ and dozens of others

As stated earlier, business analysis in the end is the business process of ensuring that the evolution of the organization mirrors the goals and objectives set by executive management. Given that lofty purpose, it is not surprising that business analysis has become a hot topic in the global marketplace today. Organizations that recognize its importance thrive regardless of their individual choice of what to call it, who actually executes it, and when they do it.

Business Analysis,
under any other name, still improves an organization's probability of success

---

More resources for you:

Self-paced Learning

View this chapter as a video for FREE
(businessanalysisexperts.com/product/what-is-business-analysis-
overview-it/)

Webinar - Bridging Business Analysis and Business Architecture
(youtube.com/watch?v=PbF_zoqo46M)

Further Reading

Strategic, Tactical, and Operational Business Analysis - *from the
author's blog*
(businessanalysisexperts.com/strategic-tactical-operational-business-analysis/)

How to Become a Business Analyst within Your Budget - *from the
author's blog*
(businessanalysisexperts.com/how-to-become-a-business-analyst/)

The Six Key Characteristics of a Senior Business Analyst
(batimes.com/kupe-kupersmith/the-six-key-characteristics-of-a-senior-
business-analyst.html)

Business Analysis: Job Title or Role - *from the author's blog*
(businessanalysisexperts.com/business-analysis-job-title-or-role/)

International Institute of Business Analysis (IIBA): What is
Business Analysis?
(iiba.org/babok-guide/babok-guide-online/chapter-one-introduction/1-2-
what-is-business-analysis.aspx)

What is the Future for Senior Business Analysts?
(batimes.com/articles/what-is-the-future-for-senior-business-analysts.html)

Thomas and Angela Hathaway

2 WHAT ARE REQUIREMENTS?

Questions answered in this chapter:

- What do we mean with requirements?
- What flavors of requirements are interesting for IT projects?

Requirements Defined

Since the primary deliverable of business analysis is a set of requirements in some form or the other, it seems like a good idea to agree on a definition of the term. In the world of business analysis, a requirement defines:

⇨ a feature that a future solution has to enable
(such as "cloud access")

⇨ a function that a future solution has to execute
(like "calculate savings")

⇨ a fact that a future solution has to enforce
(e.g., "IRS regulation XYZ")

⇨ or a quality that a future solution has to exhibit
(as in "access to a file in 1 second")

Requirements are the foundation upon which information systems are built and, just like a building, if the foundation is not solid, the building will not stand.

Fundamentally, a requirement is how we communicate what the builders (or buyers) of the solution need to build (or buy). This gets us fully into the world of human communication with all of its misunderstandings, misinterpretations, and misrepresentations.

Finally, what requirements are depends to some degree on the Software Development Methodology (SDM) that your organization uses and where in the development life cycle you are. In an Agile SDM, requirements are fundamentally negotiable whereas in a traditional (Waterfall or Iterative) SDM, changes are only allowed within a rigorous change management process.

REQUIREMENTS:

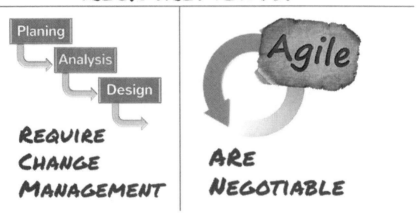

REQUIRE CHANGE MANAGEMENT | ARE NEGOTIABLE

To reduce the problems of communication between those who want a solution and those who can provide it, the International Institute for Business Analysis (**IIBA**®) in its Business Analysis Body of Knowledge™ (**BABOK**®) defines four fundamental types of requirements:

- o **Business requirements** define the goals and objectives that the organization as a whole strives to achieve.

- o **Stakeholder requirements** are the specific needs and wants of groups or individuals within the organization.

- o **Solution requirements** are the functions and qualities that a solution has to encompass to be accepted.

- o **Transition requirements** define attributes and actions necessary to implement the new solution in the existing organization.

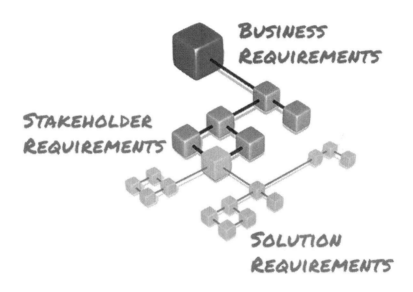

As you can see, each type of requirement expresses a different level of detail. Business requirements are very high level and a typical project will address very few. Business requirements spawn stakeholder requirements spawn solution requirements.

A typical project needs many stakeholder requirements to specify different aspects of business requirements from the perspective of the people involved. Solution requirements turn the focus of the stakeholder requirements towards the solution technology. There can be a very large number of solution requirements.

Finally, transition requirements define components of the solution that only exist to replace the current solution, as it exists today. Let us look at each type in more detail.

Business Requirements

Business requirements define high-level goals and objectives of an organization as a whole and address the question, "Why is this project needed?"

The executive level within the organization usually defines the business requirements. Their primary purpose is to prioritize and resource projects. Complete, simple sentences (potentially with collaborating explanations and cross-references), charts, and diagrams are the preferred modes for expressing business requirements. In an Agile environment, they may be expressed as "Epics", "Features", or "User Stories".

The default recommended structure for a good textual **business requirement statement** follows the mold:

To {achieve a business outcome}, {the organization or a group within} need / want / will / should {do something}.

For example,

"To maintain our leadership role within the industry, BA-EXPERTS needs to increase gross, on-line sales by 15% this fiscal year."

Or

"To increase our customer retention,
the claims department needs to reduce
claims processing time from 10 days to 4 days
by the end of the third quarter."

Stakeholder Requirements

Stakeholder requirements express the needs and wants of one or more stakeholders and how they will interact with a solution. Stakeholder requirements bridge business and solution requirements. Interviews, Joint Requirements Planning (JRP) sessions, and User Story Workshops are common tools for gathering stakeholder requirements (which should be self-authored by knowledgeable and empowered stakeholders).

Ideally, stakeholder requirements limit premature technology decisions, meaning they express what is needed not how it will be achieved. Some exceptions apply, for instance if the goal of the project is to migrate functionality to a website, the use of terms such as "online", "via the Internet", etc. are acceptable.

Stakeholder requirements can be expressed as simple statements, spreadsheets, user views, models, epics/user stories, business use cases, workflows, etc. with or without models or diagrams. A commonly used structure for a simple textual stakeholder requirement has evolved into a format known as a "User Story". Although User Stories originated in an Agile SDM, they have proven to be valuable for any SDM. They commonly follow the format:

As a {Stakeholder/Group}, I/we {can / cannot}
{do, know, or have something}
to {achieve my goal or objective}.

For example,

"As a customer, I can browse the current product catalogue to select items that I want to buy."

Or

"As a website visitor, I can view the cost of coverage for each insurance provider to select the cheapest."

Note that this structure assumes that the proposed solution already exists.

Solution Requirements

Solution requirements describe specific characteristics of a solution that meet business and stakeholder requirements and come in two flavors.

⇨ **Functional Solution Requirements**
define what the solution has to do or know.

⇨ **Non-Functional Solution Requirements**
define characteristics that any solution must exhibit for it to be acceptable.

The most common sources of solution requirements are the analysis of business and stakeholder requirements, analysis of existing IT systems, and associated stakeholder interviews (including in particular here the IT group).

Common examples for expressing **Functional Solution Requirements** are lists of functions (typically in verb/object form), solution use cases, detailed user stories, lists of data elements, prototypes or mock-ups of user views, process diagrams, data models, activity diagrams, class models, etc. Because the solution requirements are close to the technology, the representation should be easy for the developers to use.

Functional Solution Requirements include:

- The steps of a process (including sequence), decisions, alternatives, exceptions, responsibilities (e.g. "Calculate total charges including delivery costs and taxes.")

- Business rules including calculations, derivation rules, authority levels, event responses (e.g. "Do not ship goods to customers with overdue accounts.")

- Business data components including user views, relationships, meta-data (e.g. "The monthly aging report")

The most common form for expressing Non-Functional Solution Requirements are complete, simple sentences describing a quality in measurable terms.

Typical **Non-Functional Solution Requirements** address things like:

- Legal requirements

- Service level agreements

- Contractual obligations

- Audit requirements

- Internationalization requirements

- Corporate standards

- Reliability, availability, throughput, maintainability, flexibility, scalability, portability, and usability

Transition Requirements

Transition Requirements describe capabilities needed to integrate the proposed solution into the existing environment. They describe capabilities that the solution must have to facilitate getting from the as-is to the to-be but will not be needed once the new solution is in production.

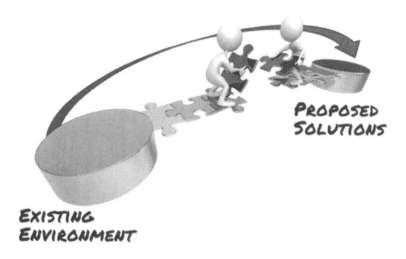

PROPOSED
SOLUTIONS

EXISTING
ENVIRONMENT

Initially defined in complete sentences, other viable forms for expressing detailed transition requirements are interfaces, database conversions, workflow designs, process models, data models, job descriptions, training programs, and job aids. A thorough understanding of the selected solution and of the current environment ultimately dictates the transition requirements. This implies that it is impossible to finalize the transition requirements before the design of the selected solution is complete.

Example of a Transition Requirement:

"Sales personnel must attend the 2-day
new customer acquisition program
prior to using the new Sales Support System."

Another example,

"All existing customer data will be maintained in both
the old and the new database format until the end of the
first quarter."

All four levels of requirements create a complete picture of the solution that both the business community and the developer community can understand.

Business requirements lead to stakeholder requirements lead to solution requirements lead to transition requirements which actually feed into new business requirements. This represents the fact that the business changes once the new solution is in use and the change will have an impact on future business requirements based on the new situation.

In addition, the risk of missing any particular category of requirements. If you remove one category of requirements, the ensuing gap represents a major risk to the success of the project. This does not imply that the number of requirements has to be enormous for the project to succeed. The volume of requirements has to be right at the right time for the size and complexity of the project and depends heavily on the level of detail they express.

The level of detail is a question of timing. In an Agile SDM, details are discussed incrementally as late as possible while in a traditional SDM they are captured in the Requirements Definition Document during the analysis phase of the project. Nonetheless, the buy-in and understanding of all requirements by the appropriate target audiences at a sufficient level of detail is crucial to implementing any viable solution.

As you can now appreciate,
the ultimate answer to the question,
"What is a requirement?"
is that it is definitely non-trivial.

More resources for you:

Self-paced Learning

View this chapter as a video for FREE
(businessanalysisexperts.com/product/what-are-business-requirements-stakeholder-solution/)

The Business Value of Better Requirements
(youtube.com/watch?v=1rtS9SmwyzA)

Three Levels of Software Requirements
(youtube.com/watch?v=VDjoiRkt06M)

eCourse: Writing Requirements in Plain English
(businessanalysisexperts.com/product/video-course-writing-requirements/)

eCourse: Requirements Analysis Destroys Ambiguity
(businessanalysisexperts.com/product/video-course-requirements-analysis-ambiguity/)

eCourse: Exposing Functional and Non-Functional Requirements
(businessanalysisexperts.com/product/video-course-exposing-functional-and-non-functional-requirements/)

eCourse: Writing User Stories
(businessanalysisexperts.com/product/video-course-writing-user-stories/)

Instructor-led Training

ILT: Requirements Elicitation – Getting User Requirements for IT Projects
(businessanalysisexperts.com/product/requirements-elicitation-gathering-business-stakeholder-it-requirements/)

3 BUSINESS ANALYSIS TECHNIQUES

Questions answered in this chapter:

- What are the primary activities in business analysis?
- What tools and techniques do they use?

An Introduction to Business Analysis Techniques

Business analysis is the process of studying a business or any other organization to identify business opportunities / problem areas and suggest potential solutions. A wide range of people with various titles, roles and responsibilities actually perform business analysis within an organization.

As we introduced in Chapter 2, "What Is Business Analysis?", there are three fundamentally different flavors or levels of business analysis:

⇨ **Strategic** Business Analysis (aka Enterprise Analysis)

⇨ **Tactical** Business Analysis

⇨ **Operational** Business Analysis

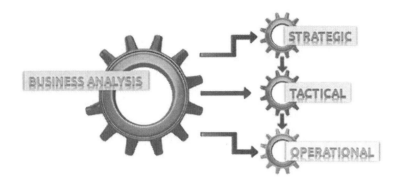

Although the activities performed at each level fall under the large "business analysis" umbrella, each level serves a different purpose. Practitioners at each level use many of the same techniques to achieve their goal, but they adjust the techniques to accommodate their target audience. Obviously, the deliverables of each level differ in the degree of detail and using tools and techniques appropriate for that level will help you achieve the desired outcome more effectively.

Strategic Business Analysis is the study of business visions, goals, objectives, and strategies of an organization or an organizational unit to identify the desired future. It encompasses the analysis of existing organizational structure, policies, politics, problems, opportunities, and application architecture to build a business case for change.

This analysis employs techniques such as:

☑ Variance Analysis

☑ Feasibility Analysis

☑ Force Field Analysis

☑ Decision Analysis

☑ and Key Performance Indicators

to support senior management in the decision-making process. The primary outcome of this work is a set of defined, prioritized projects and initiatives that the organization will undertake to create the desired future. If the initiative includes the development of software using an Agile Software Development Methodology (SDM), strategic business analysis identifies themes and/or epics, and initiates a product backlog.

Tactical Business Analysis is at the project or initiative level to flush out the details of the proposed solution and to ensure that it meets the needs of the business community.

Commonly used techniques at this level include:

- ☑ Stakeholder Identification

- ☑ Interviewing

- ☑ Facilitation

- ☑ Baselining

- ☑ Coverage Matrices

- ☑ MoSCoW Analysis

- ☑ Benchmarking

- ☑ Business Rules Analysis

- ☑ Change Management

- ☑ Process and Data Modeling

- ☑ and Functional Decomposition.

In an Agile environment, Tactical Business Analysis adds to the Product Backlog and/or Release Plans expressed in Themes, Business Epics, Architecture Epics, User Stories, and User Story Epics. In a traditional setting, the primary outcome of Tactical Business Analysis is a set of textual and/or modeled Business and Stakeholder Requirements.

Operational Business Analysts work on specific business applications. In an Agile approach, they are members of the development team and will be heavily involved in User Story elaboration and Iteration or Sprint Planning. If they are the stewards of a packaged application, they will deal primarily with identifying how to manage the application parameters to meet evolving business needs.

Their primary techniques include:

☑ Meeting Facilitation

☑ Checklist Management

☑ Prioritization

☑ Process Mapping and Analysis

☑ Business Rule Analysis

☑ Lessons Learned Analysis

☑ and Interface Analysis.

Few organizations staff all three levels of business analysis and even fewer use the terminology of **Strategic**, **Tactical**, and **Operational** Business Analyst. Regardless whether the individual tasked with defining a future IT solution has the title "Business Analyst" or not, someone on every project is "wearing the business analysis hat". The challenge for that individual is how can he or she get the job done?

Fundamentally, the one wearing the BA hat needs specific tools and/or techniques to do the job. To identify which are most suitable for the task, compare the results of two separate and unrelated surveys.

What Tools Are Used?

In search of an answer to this question, the **Requirements Solutions Group (RSG)** recently surveyed over 1700 individuals with many different job titles, all of whom wore the business analysis hat at some level of detail irrespective of the SDM their organization applied. They were asked to identify the tools they most commonly needed:

80% model and analyze business processes with tools such as Business Process Modeling Notation (BPMN), Activity Diagrams from the Unified Modeling Language (UML), and Data Flow Diagrams (DFD).

Business process analysis is the tool that uses business process models to evaluate existing or proposed business processes.

75% model and analyze business data requirements using tools such as Business Analytics, Entity/Relationship Diagrams (ERD). Business data requirements express data elements, entities, types, structures, and user views that subject matter experts need to know to be able to do their job effectively.

A business data model avoids missing data late in the project when change is extensive and expensive.

75% identify business rules as a routine part of their jobs. Business rules describe how the organization wants to conduct its business independent of the information technology.

Business rules define the behavior of an organization. If they are stored in a Rules Repository, each software application can access a common set of rules for decision-making to ensure consistency across applications.

75% do User Story and End User Acceptance Testing to ensure that the delivered IT components meet the business needs.

A User Story is a structure for expressing Stakeholder Requirements that focuses on the business use of information technology. End User Acceptance Testing is the final phase for a new or modified software application prior to rollout.

75% use backlog maintenance procedures, traceability matrices, RACI (Responsible, Accountable, Contributing, and Informed) matrices, to manage product and iteration backlogs and other forms of requirements.

Backlog maintenance refers to a practice common in environments using Agile Software Development approaches for tracking the progress of Stakeholder Requirements. Traceability matrices are more commonly used in a conventional environment. RACI matrices are a Stakeholder Analysis tool.

65% facilitate Story Workshops, Release Planning Sessions, Iteration Planning Sessions, and Requirements Discovery Workshops to identify business problems and express business, stakeholder, and solution requirements.

Story Workshops, Release Planning Session, and Iteration Planning Sessions are all tools used in an Agile Software Development Methodology. Requirements Discovery Workshops are a corollary to Story Workshops but used in a more conventional environment.

65% use Story Points, Function Points, and other estimating techniques for release planning and project scoping.

Points-based estimates are a rigorous method for predicting effort based on comparison of similar factors across projects within an organization. Story Points are predominantly used in Agile SDM while Function Points are more common in conventional environments.

55% write Business Use Cases, a specific form of functional solution requirements that focus on the interaction between the IT solution and the people using it.

A use case defines the sequence of interactions that a user of a proposed technology will execute to achieve a specified business outcome.

What Techniques Are Used?

The question then becomes, "How does THE BA do the job?" or simply "How do you do business analysis?" For an answer to that question, we offer first off a survey from the International Institute of Business Analysis (**IIBA**®). The IIBA® is an organization dedicated to defining standards and practices for the business analyst community. A 2008 survey of around 1200 business analysts asked what specific techniques business analysts needed to do their job. The responses are revealing as a list of topics that those who need to do business analysis work should know:

95% use brainstorming as a tool for business problem identification and solution definition.

Brainstorming is a general technique for eliciting many creative ideas for a target area of interest. To be effective, brainstorming sessions require an effective facilitator.

92% deal with change requests for managing requirements.

Once requirements are approved, they may be baselined, meaning that all future changes are recorded and tracked, and the current state may be compared to the baseline state. Subsequent changes to the requirement must follow a rigorous change control process.

91% need interviewing skills to elicit problems and requirements from stakeholders.

Interviewing includes all techniques needed to solicit and capture business and IT requirements using various interview approaches (1-on-1, group interviews, email interviews, etc.).

91% apply requirements-based acceptance testing.

Acceptance testing includes identifying, documenting, executing, and evaluation tests and decisions regarding the approach or methodology, tools and techniques, priorities and risks associated with the project.

89% use visual diagramming techniques such as process models, data models, activity diagrams, etc.

Process models show control and/or data flow between activities. A data model represents data entities, key attributes, relationships between entities, and the nature of those relationships. Activity diagrams are a relic of the Unified Modeling Language (UML), a standard set of diagrams associated with software products.

86% depend on a Stakeholder List as a tool for ensuring requirements completeness.

Stakeholder maps are visual diagrams that depict the relationship of stakeholders to the solution and to one another. There are many forms of stakeholder maps, but two common ones include the simple org chart and the more complex stakeholder analysis matrix.

83% identify defect/issue tracking as techniques required for their job.

Issue tracking consists of tracking error situations that arise during a walkthrough, user acceptance testing, or during the productive use of an application.

80% facilitate Requirements Workshops to ensure subject matter expert buy-in and acceptance.

Requirements workshops (e.g., JAD – Joint Application Delivery, JRP – Joint Requirements Planning, ASAP – Accelerated Systems Analysis Process, etc.) assemble a cross-functional group of subject matter experts and IT professionals with the sole purpose of creating a reasonably complete set of requirements early in the project.

Business analysts need many other techniques depending on their responsibilities in a specific organization. Examples include topics like prototyping, impact analysis, surveys/questionnaires, structured walkthroughs, document analysis, test case development, and more. Bottom line, the duties of a business analyst are non-trivial, the variety of tools and techniques used are substantial, and the amount of training needed to be effective in that role is significant.

Finally, if you are THE BA, you may need to know how to use any or all of the tools and techniques listed in either survey even if you do not have the "Business Analyst" title.

More resources for you:

Self-paced Learning

View this chapter as a video for FREE
(businessanalysisexperts.com/product/business-analysis-techniques/)

KK: Business Analysis Using User Stories
(http://businessanalysisexperts.com/product/business-analysis-using-user-stories/)

eCourse: Data Flow Diagrams Simply Put!
businessanalysisexperts.com/product/ecourse-data-flow-diagrams-context-model/)

The Business Analysis Learning Store for Anyone Wearing the Business Analysis Hat!
(http://businessanalysisexperts.com/)

Instructor-led Training

Instructor-Led Business Analysis Training from BA-EXPERTS
(businessanalysisexperts.com/product-category/business-analysis-classroom-training/)

Further Reading / Viewing

FAST TRACK to Building Business Analysis Skills
(http://businessanalysisexperts.com/fast-track-business-analysis-skills/)

Jump-Start your Business Analyst Career with a FREE Business Analysis Skills Test
(businessanalysisexperts.com/business-analyst-career-skills-test/)

How Can BASE (Business Analysis Skills Evaluation) Help You?
(businessanalysisexperts.com/business-analysis-skills-assessment-test/)

4 BUSINESS ANALYSIS AND SDM / SDLC

Questions answered in this chapter:

- What is a Software Development Methodology (SDM)?
- What changes for the THE BA?

What Are SDM and SDLC?

> An SDM (Software Development Methodology aka SDLC or Software Development Life Cycle) is a workflow for delivering and maintaining an information technology solution.

Typically, it consists of a set of activities, tasks, or steps that create one or more needed deliverables or artifacts, i.e., a requirements document, a training program, a database design, the program code, etc.). The ultimate deliverable of any SDM is a deployed or installed solution (including manual and automated components) that its intended target audience can use.

As THE BA, you are a major player in the process of defining the solution. Therefore, you need to understand how the SDM influences your requirements elicitation, specification, and documentation. Each type of SDM handles changing requirements over the life of the project differently. How do the different SDM affect your requirements definition efforts?

As the individual responsible for translating business needs into requirements at various levels of detail, you will be involved in specific aspects of the project at different times and different levels of intensity. The major differences have to do with the level of detail of the requirements, the timing of the requirements analysis and specification activities, and the form in which you document the requirements.

What Flavors of SDM Do Organizations Use?

The three different types of SDM currently in use are **Structured**, **Iterative**, and **Agile**: Structured (aka Waterfall), Iterative, and Agile development.

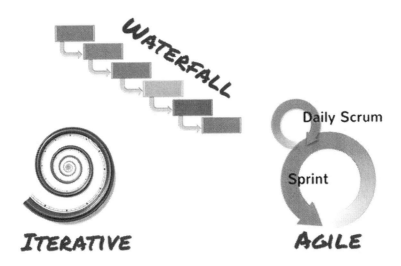

Actually, there is a fourth approach. The "Ad Hoc" (aka: Chaotic or more appropriately, "Experimental") methodology assumes you have very little knowledge of what you are doing or how to get it done. This approach is essential when a revolutionary new technology is introduced. There are no clearly defined activities or deliverables and work progresses in a "whatever needs to get done" flow. As a side note, Ad Hoc Methodologies were very popular in the 1950's and 1960's when the entire software was born and are often disparagingly referred to as the "CAL, TAL, PAL" approach ("Code a little, Test a little, Pray a lot").

CAL   TAL   PAL

Since little to nothing is known about what needs to be done when, requirements activities tend to be ad hoc, spur of the moment tasks that seldom involve a full-time business analyst. Often the need for requirements is not obvious until a fully developed solution fails to meet the customers' needs. Changing requirements often lead to considerable unscheduled rework in this approach as the customer rejects one solution after another. Due to its lack of definition, this approach is seldom referred to as a methodology.

The Beginnings of Structure

Structured or "Waterfall" approaches apply a rigorous sequence of tasks and deliverables to the process of delivering a solution. The tasks are typically subdivided into phases, such as "Planning, Analysis, Design, Development, Testing, and Deploying". Many organizations developed and sold structured methodologies in the 1970's and 1980's (e.g., Method 1, SSADM, THE Guide, etc.) and each methodology had between 5 and 9 phases. Each phase creates a major deliverable (i.e., "Business Case", "Requirements Document", "Design Specification", etc.) that can be evaluated by the appropriate authorities to reach a conscious decision whether or not to continue with the next phase.

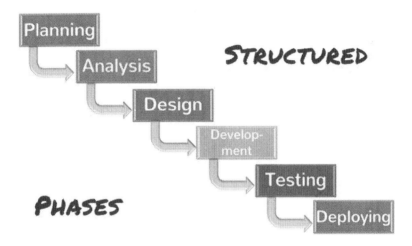

The original SDM that was developed in the 60's and set the foundation for future methodologies was called the System Development Life Cycle (SDLC). Following that philosophy, in all "structured" methodologies, the "Analysis" phase is the primary seat of business analysis activities. During this phase, requirements are elicited, documented, analyzed, and specified.

Once the deliverable of the "Analysis" phase has been accepted, changes to the requirements undergo impact analysis based on a rigorous Change Management protocol. THE BA should be and is typically a member of the change review board.

The Incremental Philosophy

Due to the challenges (and associated costs) that changing requirements posed to structured methodologies, the idea of "Iterative" (aka "Spiral" or "Incremental") software development emerged in the '70's and '80's.

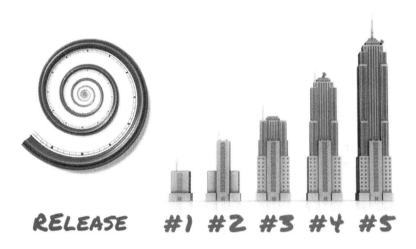

Iterative approaches assume that while the overall project goals and objectives remain relatively constant, the development of the solution will cause the needs to change and that will require modifications to the delivered solution. Iterative methodologies break the tasks of delivering IT solutions into smaller chunks and break the project into a series of "releases". Each release provides a piece of the final solution that the user community can use. Subsequent releases "morph" the solution to add features and functions that will ultimately lead to a complete solution.

Typically, iterative methodologies divide the tasks into **four phases**:

1. Inception,
2. Elaboration,
3. Construction,
4. and Transition or some similar names.

The Inception phase is the initiation of the project and only occurs once. The remaining three phases overlap and are repeated for each release. Most business analysis activities will take place during the Inception and Elaboration phases.

Because iterative methodologies deliver the final product over time in a series of releases, the focus of the requirements is release specific. That means that while THE BA captures high-level business and stakeholder requirements for the project in the Inception phase, detailed analysis and specification of the requirements is done for each iteration during the Elaboration phase focusing on the requirements for that release.

An "Agile" Revolution

The Agile approach is a child of the 21st century. The idea and the founding principles are based on the "Agile Manifesto". It takes the iterative concept to the extreme and assumes a state of constant change. Agile projects manage change by maintaining an on-going communication between the "business community" and the "developer community". It recognizes that requirements cannot always be defined at the beginning of the project but need to be reevaluated and refined on a daily basis.

Many Agile approaches are in use today. One of the most popular is the "Scrum" approach that involves brief, daily meetings to discuss progress and establish expectations. An Agile team consists primarily of developers and representatives of the business community. It includes a full-time Business Analyst if the complexity of the solution warrants it. Otherwise, the product owner, developers, and testers wear the business analysis hat when and where needed.

High-level business requirements need to be articulated and agreed upon before the project can be initiated. Specific requirements in the form of "User Stories" are collected into a "Product Backlog" and are analyzed and specified immediately before developers start to work on them. Work is planned in a series of "Releases" and "Sprints" with each delivering some form of value to the customer. Documentation in Agile projects tends to be minimal and is often discarded as soon as the immediate need is satisfied.

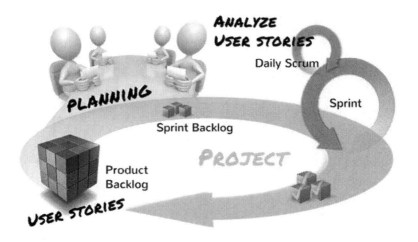

As THE BA, you will most likely not be able to select the ideal methodology for your project. However, you should be aware of how the selected methodology influences your business analysis activities on the project. For that purpose. let us look at each approach from the perspective of how it will impact your business analysis activities when you are THE BA.

Business Analysis in Waterfall SDM

Waterfall methodologies treat the software development process as a manufacturing or construction process. Progress is viewed as a steady flow from project initiation through analysis, design, development, testing, and delivery.

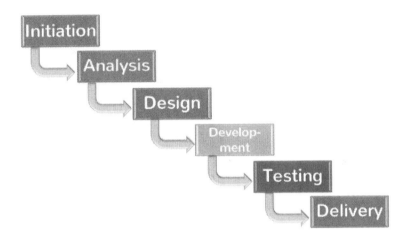

During the initiation of the project, THE BA might be involved in creating a business case. The skill set for this activity includes problem analysis, goals and objectives definition, cost-benefit analysis, and presentation to senior management. These activities fall into the Strategic Business Analysis category defined earlier, implying a need for a high degree of business analysis skills.

In the Analysis phase, THE BA's responsibility is the creation of a Requirements Definition Document (or RDD for short) or something similar. During this phase, significant effort goes into requirements definition and analysis to capture, clarify, and confirm the requirements. THE BA elicits and analyzes business and stakeholder needs which are expressed in natural language and/or models. Process and data models are typical of waterfall methodologies and enhance communication between the various stakeholders on the project which can lead to early identification of potentially volatile areas. These activities are representative of the Tactical Business Analysis category, meaning THE BA needs a fair degree of business analysis skills.

In the design phase of the project, THE BA together with Subject Matter Experts (SME's) and developers defines solution and transition requirements as well as technical specifications. This is actually the domain of Operational business analysis.

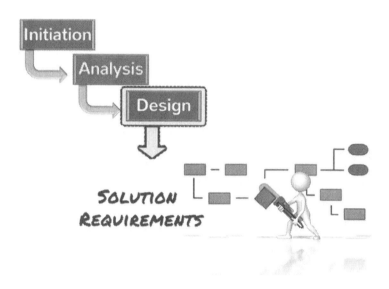

Any changes that arise after acceptance of a phase are managed with varying degrees of success through a rigorous "Change Management" process. The role of business analysis is most clearly defined and delineated in the Waterfall approach. THE BA is a major player during the Analysis phase of the project. The premise is that it is possible to clearly define most if not all stakeholder requirements during this phase. It is assumed that THE BA will define solution requirements as complete as possible during the design phase. Since it is unrealistic to expect that nothing will change, THE BA will also typically be responsible for managing changes to the requirements throughout the life of the project.

Professional business analysts are usually responsible for Requirements Management activities in which the requirements are traced back to problems as well as through all process models, data models, and all other project artifacts. Requirements Management effort in the waterfall method is very high but absolutely necessary to deal cost-effectively with changes in requirements during the development of the project (and the IT industry found out the hard way that it cannot live without changing requirements).

Although testing is not a recognized business analysis activity, many organizations also assign the responsibility for acceptance testing to THE BA. This is presumably based on the recognition that no one understands the requirements better than THE BA does. If you are in this situation, you need an entirely different set of skills to effectively verify and validate that the delivered software actually does what the business community requested.

THE BA Role in Iterative SDM

Iterative methodologies assume that change will happen and plan for it. A widespread Iterative methodology is IBM's Rational Unified Process (or RUP). A major feature of the Iterative approach is the assumption that the ultimate solution will be created in a series of releases or iterations. Your role as THE BA in Iterative methodologies in each phase is similar to your role in the waterfall approaches.

The initial phase of any project is the "Inception" phase. During this phase, THE BA will elicit and capture the vision statement and high-level business goals and objectives. You might create the business case for the project using problem analysis, cost benefit analysis, and business and stakeholder requirements definition techniques.

The project is then broken down into a series of iterations, each of which has a single key objective. Each iteration goes through potentially multiple "Elaboration", "Construction", and "Transition" phases to ultimately deliver a release that represents a "preliminary version" of the final product.

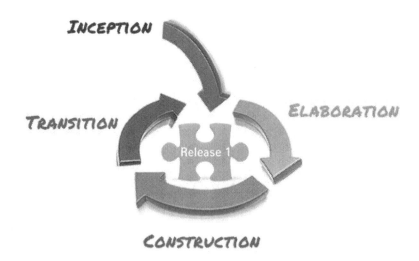

In the Elaboration phase, THE BA defines solution requirements. One of the major techniques that has evolved to support object-oriented system development and by association Iterative methodologies is the Unified Modeling Language (UML). The UML is a highly complex set of diagramming symbols, making it relatively difficult to learn and requiring highly abstract thinking. Developers use it heavily in the software development process on a regular basis but, due to its complexity, the UML is seldom used in the business analysis arena.

One exception to that rule is the use of a concept called Use Cases. Business Use Cases are a very common documentation method for capturing the solution requirements for an evolving information technology solution. A major attribute of the Use Case is the focus on a single usage of the application by a single user. This gives THE BA a phenomenal tool for expressing functional requirements. By design, the UML allows for extensions giving it a great degree of flexibility and giving THE BA the opportunity to add dimensions to cover the requirements component.

Furthermore, in the Elaboration phase, THE BA together with the Subject Matter Experts (SMEs) develops prototypes if needed and, sometimes, creates preliminary user manuals. It is also THE BA's responsibility in this phase to have agreement from all stakeholders regarding the requirements. In the Construction phase THE BA has to be available to the developers for any requirements clarifications that are needed. In the transition phase, THE BA might be tasked with acceptance testing tasks such as creating test plans, test cases, and test scripts. Whether or not THE BA is involved in testing is an organizational decision.

A fundamental business analysis task in this phase is to define transition requirements and help the development team to "transition" the system from development to production. After completion of the transition phase, the next iteration for this project starts and all business analysis activities are repeated.

Agile Projects and Business Analysis

Agile is an approach to delivering information technology (IT) solutions that focuses on changing business needs and technologies. The founding group published its premise and promise on the web in 2001 as "The Agile Manifesto", declaring (amongst other things):

⇨ Our highest priority is to satisfy the customer through early and continuous delivery of valuable software.

⇨ Welcome changing requirements, even late in development.

⇨ Business people and developers must work together DAILY throughout the project.

⇨ The most efficient and effective method of conveying information to and within a development team is face-to-face conversation.

⇨ Simplicity — the art of maximizing the amount of work not done — is essential.

This means that THE BA on an Agile project does business analysis strictly on an as-needed basis. However, as with every other methodology, some degree of up-front definition of business vision, goals, objectives, and high-level stakeholder requirements ("Strategic Business Analysis") is essential.

Of all available methodologies, Agile is the approach most receptive to change. Nothing is permanent until the project has delivered a solution that is "sufficient to the needs of the users". There are several Agile methodologies available. Currently, the most well-known are Scrum, Lean, Kanban, eXtreme Programming (XP), Crystal, Dynamic Systems Development Method (DSDM), and Feature-Driven Development (FDD). As of 2012, about 74% of Agile projects follow the Scrum approach or are Scrum/XP hybrids.

The SCRUM approach divides software development into small chunks known as "Sprints", each of which deliver a working piece of software (aka: incremental functionality). An "Iteration" is a series of

Sprints which taken together deliver a software component that provides business value to the customer.

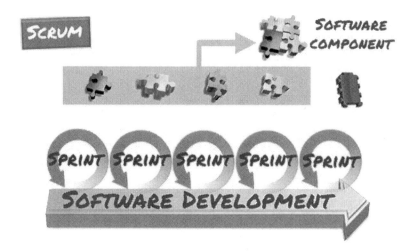

One distinguishing characteristic of all Agile methodologies is the lack of distinction between phases such as Analysis, Design, Coding, and Testing. All of these activities occur iteratively within the Sprint. In the Scrum and Scrum/XP hybrids, the major mode for expressing requirements is the User Story. A User Story describes what the system needs to do for a specific user role and why the user needs it. The Agile team creates a set of tasks for each User Story to be able to estimate and coordinate individual work.

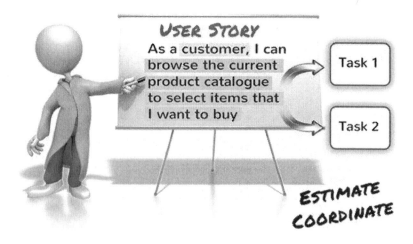

In Agile, as in every other methodology, a project starts with some form of a vision. The vision can be in someone's head (in which case someone needs to formulate and communicate it to the team) or any other form of representation. Formal business goals and objectives or an official "Vision Statement" are common forms.

Regardless how your organization expresses it, it has to define:

☑ What business problem(s) the project will solve

☑ What the business goals and objectives are

☑ What features and benefits will be provided

☑ Who will be the recipient of the solution

It may also include statements about performance, reliability, platforms, standards, applications, etc. One of the first steps in Agile development is to create an initial "Backlog", commonly called a "Product Backlog", "Kanban board", "Feature Set", or something similar depending on the specific methodology. The Product Owner is ultimately responsible for maintaining the Backlog which is initially seeded from an analysis of the vision. Due to the nature of this work, THE BA is often tasked with it.

Depending on the maturity of the Agile team, the Backlog can contain anything from business goals and objectives, Business Requirements, "Themes", "Features", "Epics", etc. to Stakeholder Requirements at any level of detail (commonly in User Story format). The Agile team uses the Backlog to plan Iterations and Sprints. Pinpointing the exact level of detail is not necessary early in the project because THE BA (again, whoever is wearing the Business Analysis hat) will do that in more detail during the Iteration or Sprint planning sessions on an as-needed basis.

The Backlog lives. THE BA adds new and changing User Stories and/or Work Items throughout the project. The Agile Team prioritizes the Backlog often to ensure that they are working on what are at that time the highest priorities for the project. Requirements within a Sprint are often quite informal and undocumented. The most formal requirements in Scrum/XP approaches are User Stories written on index cards or maintained in an electronic system. Notes scribbled on a cocktail napkin (which THE BA can scan as documentation, if necessary) are also an acceptable form.

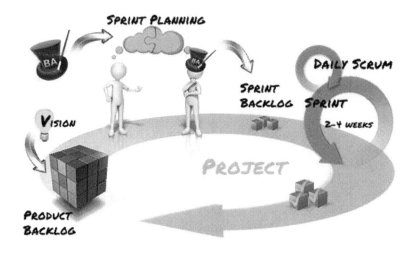

Your involvement as THE BA will depend on the specific Agile methodology chosen. With Scrum and Scrum/XP hybrids, typical Agile Teams consist of the specific roles:

o   Product Owner or customer representative (who is or has access to THE BA)

o   a Scrum/Agile Master

o   Developers

o   Testers

It is interesting to note that each individual's role on an Agile project is fluid and can change as the need changes. This mandates a high degree of flexibility and a broad set of skills of each team member, each of whom may become THE BA at different times in the project. To be successful, THE BA needs a versatile set of tools for eliciting requirements on the fly.

Ideally, the entire Agile team is physically co-located to satisfy the Agile premise regarding face-to-face communication. Geographically dispersed teams can use virtual presence to come as close as possible to physical co-location.

Although the techniques for specifying (aka drill-down, decomposing or flushing out) Stakeholder Requirements in Agile are much the same as in any other development approach, the timing and level of detail are VERY different. It is a true balancing act between making sure that the requirements are "good enough" to ensure that all stakeholders in a project are fully satisfied while avoiding any unnecessary business analysis activities or techniques.

In Agile, THE BA facilitates the process of defining, analyzing, comprehending, organizing, optimizing, testing, and integrating the requirements for a given Sprint. Ultimately, the entire team is responsible for deciding whether decomposed User Stories are sufficient or the team requires techniques that are more elaborate. The team may have to create Activity Diagrams, process models, data models, State Diagrams, or other models to communicate the intent of the requirements and not just the words.

Once the developers have built and tested a User Story, it has to undergo Acceptance Testing. In many organizations, this is the responsibility of THE BA. In some Agile teams, THE BA also creates and executes test cases and scripts for the developers as part of Unit Testing. THE BA may also be responsible for generating testing reports for the developers.

As of 2013, the Agile approach is rapidly becoming the methodology of choice for many IT projects. Proven successes on projects of suitable size is a major contributing factor. According to industry studies published in 2011, Agile projects are more than twice as likely to succeed as compared with those using a structured or spiral approach. Until recently, the team-driven nature of the Agile approach has constrained the size of projects for which it is likely to succeed. However, as organizations and the IT industry gain more experience with Agile, they are constantly pushing the size envelope. At the current time, the Agile team approach is best suited for dealing with the complexity and rate of change inherent in modern information technology development.

Any SDM will work for any project.
The critical question is how well-suited
the two are for each other?

More resources for you:

Self-paced Learning

View this chapter as videos for FREE
(businessanalysisexperts.com/product/business-analysis-sdm-system-
development-methodologies/
businessanalysisexperts.com/product/business-analysis-agile-methodologies/
businessanalysisexperts.com/product/business-analyst-waterfall-
methodologies/)

Agile Product Ownership in a Nutshell
(youtube.com/watch?v=502ILHjX9EE)

Backlog Refinement Meeting
(youtube.com/watch?v=b_WeHcZcx1w)

What is a 'Product Owner'? - Scrum Guide
(youtube.com/watch?v=3eljozEWpf8)

Requirements Gathering and Change Management in Agile vs.
Waterfall (Cherifa Mansoura from IBM)
(youtube.com/watch?v=sPOSYqT-1eY)

Further Reading

Agile Extension to the BABOK® Guide
(iiba.org/BABOK-Guide/Agile-Extension-to-the-BABOK-Guide-IIBA.aspx)

What Is an Agile Business Analyst?
(batimes.com/steve-blais/what-is-an-agile-business-analyst.html)

5 BUSINESS ANALYSIS AND THE FUTURE

Questions answered in this chapter:

- Where do we see business analysis going?
- How will that affect you?

Existing Situation Analysis

So what can the future of Business Analysis look like? Using the power that is unique to human minds, we are going to explore likely scenarios to provide a reasonable response to the question. To predict the future, we need to find relevant similar situations in the past.

Until recent, the job title "Business Analyst" did not exist and even today, the actual duties of those with the job title "Business Analyst" vary widely from one organization to the next. In some organizations, the business analyst is an entry-level position responsible only for writing down requests from subject matter experts and transmitting those to the developer community. In other organizations, the business analyst is a very senior position instrumental in defining the future strategies of the organization and everyone in it. Many of these "Senior BAs" report directly to the CEO or President of the organization.

Practicing business analysts today may have a background in system analysis but recognize the importance of understanding the business processes and procedures in detail before changing the supporting technology. Based on what we see in corporate America attending our training, however, a large percentage of those with the title "Business Analyst" come out of the business community. These are often the "Super-Users" of the existing applications who recognize areas for improvement and want to actively contribute to finding solutions that

work for their colleagues.

In the first section of this book, we introduced the concepts of "Strategic", "Tactical", and "Operational" business analysis. The roles and responsibilities of business analysts in today's world span the entire spectrum and sometimes an individual is expected to wear all three of these very different-sized hats.

Regardless of where they came from, practicing business analysts tend to recognize that they need to expand their repertoire of analysis techniques to be proficient at their job. Actually, they are applying their natural analysis skills to their own environment and identifying problem areas in need of fixing. Simply put, they are requesting (and in many cases getting) professional training in some of the techniques listed in the previous chapter.

Core Business Analysis Competencies

The primary skills anyone doing business analysis needs can be grouped into these categories:

- ☑ The courage to ask anyone tough questions and challenge the status quo.

- ☑ The imagination to look at any existing situation critically and identify core questions that needed to be asked to ferret out issues.

- ☑ The ability to analyze a set of facts and recognize problems or areas in need of improvement.

- ☑ The language to define criteria that any potential solution must have to resolve the identified issues.

- ☑ The rigor to follow up with validating that the delivered solution meets the defined criteria.

Note that none of these require computer expertise. They also do not require any specific business acumen. Viewed from that perspective, it becomes apparent that these abilities are valuable to anyone in any profession, whether the problems they are addressing are related to business processes, child raising, medical procedures, nutrition, nuclear physics, or anything else. As a result, what we have defined here as "business analysis" is rapidly becoming acknowledged as core skills that anyone needs to survive in the 21st century.

From Niche Profession to Core Skillset

Business analysis is fundamentally a way of thinking. Organizations that have recognized this are reacting appropriately. Many are no longer trying to fill "Business Analyst" positions per se but are looking for candidates who can do business analysis as part of their "real" job. In antiquity, only a select few had the ability to capture knowledge in written form. Reading and mathematics were also not taught to commoners.

It is dubious that the position of business analyst will disappear anytime soon. More likely, the evolving distinction between "Strategic" and "Operational" business analysis will lead organizations to employ a small number of "Super BAs" who are tasked with the strategic component and people throughout the organization who have the necessary skills will perform the operational level. The tactical component will most likely be staffed with resources from the other two pools depending on the nature of the specific undertaking.

Reading, Writing, and Business Analysis?

It is time to add a fourth dimension to the basic skills every person should start acquiring at a young age. To succeed in business and in life in the future, people really need four core skills, namely "Reading, Writing, Arithmetic, AND Analysis". Whether you use these skills in your chosen profession or in your personal life, you will be able to define – and ultimately create – a better future on a more conscious level.

Bottom line, you may be doing
'business analysis' already and not know it.
If you enjoy it, maybe you should consider
some training to hone your inherent skills and allow
you to make more efficient use of them.

More resources for you:

Self-paced Learning

FREE Business Analysis Training Videos

(businessanalysisexperts.com/product-category/free-business-analysis-training/)

Business Analysis eCourses

(businessanalysisexperts.com/product-category/self-paced-business-analysis-courses-online/)

Further Reading

The Future is Now: The 21st Century Enterprise Business Analyst

(batimes.com/kathleen-hass/the-future-is-now-the-21st-century-enterprise-business-analyst.html)

The Future of Business Analysis - IIBA

(iiba.org/Learning-Development/Webinars/Public-Archive/2012/Encore-Presentation.aspx)

Where is the Business Analysis Profession Going?

(batimes.com/articles/where-is-the-business-analysis-profession-going.html)

2014 Trends in Business Analysis and Project Management

(batimes.com/elizabeth-larson/2014-trends-in-business-analysis-and-project-management.html)

Business Analysis: Top Trends

(insights.dice.com/top-trends-in-business-analysis/)

Tales of Future Past

(iiba.org/ba-connect/2014/january/tales-of-future-past.aspx)

The End of Business Analysis or a Top Career to Pursue? - *from the author's blog*

(businessanalysisexperts.com/the-end-of-business-analysis/)

ABOUT THE AUTHORS

Angela and Tom Hathaway have authored and delivered hundreds of training courses and publications for business analysts around the world. They have facilitated hundreds of requirements discovery sessions for information technology projects under a variety of acronyms (JAD, ASAP, JADr, JRP, etc.).

Based on their personal journey and experiences reported by their students, they recognized how much anyone can benefit from a basic understanding of what is currently called "business analysis". Their mission is to allow everyone, anywhere access to simple, easy-to-learn techniques by sharing their experience and expertise in their training seminars, blogs, books, and public presentations.

Thomas and Angela Hathaway

Made in the USA
Columbia, SC
18 October 2017